GET A JOB AT THE CONSTRUCTION SITE

JOE RHATIGAN

Created and produced by
Bright Futures Press, Cary, North Carolina
www.brightfuturespress.com

Published by
Cherry Lake Publishing, Ann Arbor, Michigan
www.cherrylakepublishing.com

Photo Credits: cover, Shutterstock/Frank L Junior; page 4, Shutterstock/ivrii; page 5, Dmitry Kalinovsky; page 7, Shutterstock/Rido; page 7, Shutterstock/vovan; page 9, Shutterstock/Blend Images; page 11, Shutterstock/Milos Stojanovic; page 11, Shutterstock/Phovoir; page 13, Shutterstock/Andresr; page 15, Shutterstock/SusaZoom; page 15, Shutterstock/wi6995; page 17, Shutterstock/Kzenon; page 19, Shutterstock/surauid; page 19, Shutterstock/Kzenon; page 21, Shutterstock/Cynthia Farmer; page 23, Shutterstock/Dmitry Kalinovsky; page 23, Shutterstock/Phovoir; page 25, Shutterstock/Racheal Grazias; page 26, Shutterstock/Andresr; page 27, Shutterstock/Naypong; page 28, Shutterstock/Dmitry Kalinovsky.

Illustrated by Chris Griffin

Library of Congress Cataloging-in-Publication Data

Names: Rhatigan, Joe, author.
Title: Get a job at a construction site / by Joe Rhatigan.
Description: Ann Arbor, Michigan : Cherry Lake Publishing, 2016. | Series: Get a job | Audience: Grades 4-6. | Includes index.
Identifiers: LCCN 2016006910| ISBN 9781634719049 (hardcover) | ISBN 9781634719506 (pbk.) | ISBN 9781634719278 (pdf) | ISBN 9781634719735 (ebook)
Subjects: LCSH: Building--Juvenile literature. | Construction workers--Juvenile literature. | School buildings--Design and construction--Juvenile literature.
Classification: LCC TH159 .R534 2016 | DDC 690--dc23
LC record available at http://lccn.loc.gov/2016006910

Printed in the United States of America

TABLE OF CONTENTS

Have you ever passed a construction site?

You may have seen many men and women with hard hats and tool belts on. Maybe they were moving things around, pouring concrete, or looking over blueprints. You may think that there's no way this new building will ever be completed. Yet day by day, week by week, the building goes up. It's amazing!

For some people, watching from afar is fun. For others, getting up close is a must. And so it is with the curious and clumsy **J**eremiah **O**liver **B**aumgartner. The kid's initials are J.O.B., so his friends call him Job for short. His parents like his nickname because sometimes it is hard work parenting a kid like Job.

As much as he enjoys watching the construction of his new school from his math classroom window, he wants to be closer—a lot closer. So with his math teacher's help, he forms a club called the Construction Crew. Each month a few kids and "Mr. Tony" are allowed to tour the site and watch the construction people build their school.

Read on and you'll learn a lot about many of the fun and challenging jobs at a construction site. Unlike Job, you can leave your hard hat at home ... for now.

BUILDER BITS

More than 6 million people work i construction in the United States.

HAPTER 1

JOB JOINS THE CONSTRUCTION CREW

"But why do we need a bus?" Job asked as the Construction Crew left the school and headed downtown. "We could easily walk to the site."

"Yes," Mr. Tony said, "but we're not going to the site."

Job was confused. "But I want to wear my new hard hat, safety goggles, and reflective vest."

Mr. Tony then told the group that there were many people who worked behind the scenes planning how to build the new school.

"Okay, but can I still wear my safety gear?" Job asked.

"Job, you're so clumsy that you should always wear safety gear!" Mr. Tony laughed.

Just then the bus stopped short, and Job bumped his head on the seat in front of him.

"I see what you mean," Job said.

The Crew got to sit in on a meeting that included many of the planners of the new school. The construction manager sat at the head of the table and is in charge of the entire process of constructing a building. The **construction manager** works closely with the building owner and architect to make sure the building that is built is the building they want.

The **architect** designs spaces where people live, work, and play and creates detailed plans that guide the construction process. The architect designs the outside of the building and all the inside rooms—even showing where doors, windows, and other features are to be located.

Architects plan every detail of a building.

The **interior designer** is in charge of designing the inside spaces of buildings, including lighting, fixtures, color schemes, furniture, and appliances. It is the designer's job to make sure the inside space of a building works well and looks good too. The interior designer consults with clients to get a sense of their needs and design preferences, creates concept drawings, and makes sure that the end result is exactly what the client requested.

Drafters use special computer software, called computer-aided designer or CAD, to turn the architect's designs into technical drawings or **blueprints**. Workers at the construction site use these drawings to build the intended structure.

Computer-aided design can be used to make 3-D images.

BUILDER BITS

The tallest building in the world (so far) is Burj Khalifa, a skyscraper in Dubai. It is 2,717 feet tall.

Cost estimators are in charge of the money. They create budgets for everyone involved in the project and make sure that nobody spends too much money as they rent equipment, buy materials, and hire **contractors** to build the school.

THE RESULTS

After meeting with the building planners and looking over the blueprints of the new school, Job decided that construction could be fun even without safety gear.

However, it did come in handy when Job had trouble with the water fountain.

And when he knocked over the blueprints.

And when he tripped over a backpack.

Everyone at the meeting thought it wise to keep Job AWAY from the construction site at all costs.

CHAPTER 2

JOB AND THE CONSTRUCTION SITE

A few weeks later, the Construction Crew headed to the site with Mr. Tony.

Several large trucks and loaders were busy removing the concrete from the parking lot that used to be at the site. Other machines were digging the basement where the school's lunchroom would be located. Once again, Job was disappointed that he didn't need his safety gear since nobody was allowed inside the fenced area. But he was happy that he brought along his ear protectors because it was LOUD.

Mr. Tony gave Job a pair of binoculars and said, "This is as close as we're getting today."

"What?" Job asked.

"We will meet with a few people who are getting the site ready for building," Mr. Tony continued.

"Huh?" Job asked.

"TAKE OFF THOSE EAR PROTECTORS!" everybody yelled at once.

"Okay," Job said. "But you don't have to yell!"

The first person they met was the **safety officer**. Construction can be a dangerous job, which is why many sites hire safety officers. A safey officer's job is to keep the workers (and any visitors) safe while on-site. The safety officer performs inspections and watches to see that the workers are following the safety rules and wearing the proper gear. Safety officers report any problems and train workers on the proper ways to get the job done.

Excavators dig deep foundations and basements.

The **excavation manager** met with the kids next. He directs a team of earth-moving workers to dig trenches for building **foundations**, basements, and other construction. He manages the process of removing any trees and making sure the environment (soil, water, and wildlife) is properly protected while digging.

Job could see someone with what looked like a camera tripod taking pictures. This is the **surveyor**, who uses measurement tools to place markers that will guide the construction process. These markers will tell workers where to build the road leading up to a building as well as where to precisely locate the building. Surveyors must know geometry and other higher math subjects like physics and engineering. They also need to know how to use very specialized equipment.

Surveyors mark boundaries.

BUILDER BITS

Construction cranes were invented by the Ancient Greeks. They were powered by men or donkeys.

The Crew could see many large machines being operated on the site. The cranes, front loaders, bulldozers, load lifters, and diggers are operated by **heavy equipment operators**. These men and women are trained to use one or more of the large machines to dig, grade, move, and lift heavy and large items. Workers usually sit in the cab and use pedals, levers, switches, and dials to control the machine.

The one thing every construction site needs is workers—lots of workers. These are people who may not have a lot of experience but can lift, move, measure, build, dig, and do all the physical labor needed. **Construction workers** do all that and more. A general construction worker will assist with loading and unloading materials, digging ditches, operating small equipment, and cleanup.

THE RESULTS

Job loved meeting the safety officer and was pleased when she complimented him on his safety gear.

"Maybe next time, you can all tour the actual site," she said.

"Will we need any extra safety gear?" Job asked.

"Well, from what I hear about you, a suit of armor might be a smart choice."

Job put on his ear protectors as everyone laughed.

CHAPTER 3
JOB GETS A HARD HAT

The next time the Crew visited the site, most of the heavy equipment was gone and much of the materials were where they needed to be.

So this time, the safety officer gave the kids permission to venture inside the site. The foundation of the building had been poured, and the frame was beginning to take shape.

"Where's the kid with all the safety gear?" she asked. "I want him to lead the way."

Of course, this time Job had left all his safety gear at home.

"Um ... the dog ate it," he said sadly.

But no worries—each kid got his own hard hat, and Job's fit him perfectly.

Concrete finishers pour wet cement into molds or forms in order to create foundation slabs, sidewalks, roads, and other projects. They must be able to figure out how much concrete is needed for the job and how to best mix the sand and cement. They will also place reinforcements in the concrete such as **rebar** or wire mesh to make the concrete stronger. Finally, they will keep an eye on the poured concrete as it hardens, make sure it is level or at the correct grade, and apply sealants to keep it waterproof.

If any stone will be used in the construction, then a **stone mason** will be needed. Stone masons start with rough pieces of rock or stone. They use a hammer, chisel, and sometimes even a **blowtorch** to shape and combine the stones in order to create a structure such as a building.

Stone masons use stones to make walkways.

A **brick mason** uses bricks, concrete blocks, and other stones to build walls of buildings and other structures. Brick masons mix mortar for spreading on a slab or foundation and then precisely place bricks or blocks according to the blueprints. Brick masons use levels and plumb bobs to make sure all their measurements are exact. Even a small mistake could result in having to start all over again.

As a building goes up, a **welder** is called upon whenever two pieces of metal need to be joined together. Welders use their knowledge of metals to cut, position, and then—using an electric current or other method—combine the two pieces. Welders are exposed to intense and blinding heat and have to wear special gloves, aprons, and a mask to prevent burns.

Welders need protective gear to avoid injuries.

BUILDER BITS

You could build a highway from New York City to San Francisco with the concrete needed to build the Hoover Dam.

If a building is made mostly of wood, a carpenter known as a **framer** is called. Framers build the frame of the building using different types of wood beams and lumber. Tools needed include handsaws, power saws, and woodworking machines. When framers are done, the building will look like a skeleton, with the frame for the floors, walls, and roof constructed—but little else.

THE RESULTS

After the tour, Job decided he wanted to be a welder.

"Why is that?" Mr. Tony asked.

"Well, I really like making things ... and ..."

Before he could finish, his classmates chimed in, "He loves the safety mask!"

Sure enough, that's exactly what Job was thinking.

HAPTER 4

JOB GOES INSIDE OUT

After a few months, the building looked nearly finished.

The walls were up, and the windows had been installed. The roof was almost complete.

"It looks like it's ready for students," Job said.

"Well," Mr. Tony said, "just because something looks like it's done doesn't mean it's done. Sort of like your math homework."

And during their next trip, the Construction Crew could see that their new school was still a construction site and not quite ready for business. There were still lots of people lifting, hammering, and moving. The workers they met all had very specific jobs that took skill and hard work.

The Crew first met the **construction inspector**, who was examining the construction site to make sure the builders were following code and pulling proper **permits**. It's an important job that requires attention to detail so that once the building is finished, it will pass all of its safety inspections. This job requires a good knowledge of construction methods, electrical and mechanical systems, and the area's building regulations.

Then the kids saw several people carefully carrying large pieces of glass into the building. They were **glaziers**, who specialize in cutting, installing, and sealing glass for skylights and other unusually shaped windows. They also provide the glass for office doors, trophy cases, mirrors, and tabletops.

Glaziers make precise cuts so windows fit.

Drywall installers were carrying large rectangular pieces of drywall—also known as plasterboard—into the building. Drywall is a panel made of plaster pressed between two thick sheets of paper. It is used to make inside walls and ceilings. Drywall installers fasten these drywall panels to the inside frame of the building. These are the walls for all the rooms, so they must be smooth, seamless, and ready to be prepped for painting or wallpapering.

On the roof, they saw several workers applying tar and shingles to the top of the building. **Roofers** specialize in building a structure's roof. They analyze the construction plans and make sure the roof is constructed exactly according to the plan. Roofers choose the materials best suited for the building so that bad weather doesn't make it inside.

Carpenters use a variety of hand tools.

BUILDER BITS

It took 10 million bricks, 60,000 tons of steel, and 200,000 cubic feet of limestone and granite to build the Empire State Building in New York City.

Finally, several **finish carpenters** were working both inside and outside the building. They create cabinets, trim and moldings, doors, windows, mantels, and other decorative wood elements that help rooms look special. Finish carpenters might create fancy bannisters for the stairwells, useful cubbies for the younger grades, and even furniture for the teachers' lounge. Some finish carpenters starts out as a rough carpenters where they learn how to cut, measure, and use hand tools.

THE RESULTS

At this point, the big trucks were gone, although the grounds around the building were sloppy and muddy. The kids were allowed to walk the hallways, visit the classrooms, and even walk through the gymnasium, although they still had to wear their hard hats.

All the people they had met needed a lot of knowledge—especially math—and skill to do their jobs.

This reminded Job of the homework he had to complete FULLY by tomorrow.

HAPTER 5

JOB SEES HIS NEW SCHOOL

It was nearly the end of the school year, and the new school building had lights, heat and air conditioning, and even grass around the front entrance.

The trucks coming and going from the new school reminded Job of his own house.

"When I break stuff, a repair person has to come and fix it," Job said. "Are these guys fixing things at the new school?"

"No, Job," Mr. Tony said. "They are either installing equipment or putting the finishing touches on what they are working on."

"Oh. I bet some of those guys know me," Job said.

"I'm sure they do, Job. I'm sure they do."

Electricians are involved in the construction process from the very beginning. These tradespeople are responsible for all the wiring of the new building. They install electrical systems and fix problems as they test the wiring before the building is ready for business. Working from the blueprints, they make sure all the rooms have the electricity needed for lights, appliances, computers, and more.

Like the electricians, **plumbers** have been part of the process from the beginning. They install water and drainage pipes for all the kitchens and bathrooms, and they make sure to follow the blueprints and building codes.

Electricians wire buildings for power.

The **painters** and **paperhangers** are doing just what their name suggests: painting and hanging wallpaper. Some don't have a lot of experience and will spend time learning from a trained professional. Others will have more experience and can work neatly and quickly from room to room doing a professional job.

A **landscape architect** creates designs and prepares models for the outside spaces and parks of a building, home, or school campus. **Landscapers** follow plans created by a landscape architect and plant the bushes, trees, and other plants around the building in a pleasing way.

Plumbers get water into and out of buildings.

In many circumstances, Job noticed that one or more of these tradespeople seemed to

BUILDER BITS

The longest structure ever built is the Great Wall of China. It stretches nearly 4,000 miles.

be in charge and the others working with them were being told what to do. These workers are **apprentices**—people who learn how to do a jobs by helping experts in the field. Many of these workers don't need a college degree to do their jobs but they may take classes at a **trade school** to learn job skills.

THE RESULTS

"This is our last visit to the building," Mr. Tony said.

Most of the kids were excited to finally see their new school ready for students and teachers. The classrooms had whiteboards and fancy new desks. The lunchroom was twice as big as the old one, and the kitchen was brand new. Best of all, the yard outside looked perfect for freeze tag. Job, however, looked a little sad.

"What's the matter, Job? Don't you like how it turned out?" Mr. Tony asked.

"Well," Job said, "I'm not sure I like this building anymore."

"Why not?" his teacher asked in astonishment.

"It was great watching it get built and all. But now, it feels way too much like ... school!"

CHAPTER 6
WHO DOES WHAT AT THE CONSTRUCTION SITE?

WHO DOES WHAT?

Job met some interesting people during his visits to the construction site. Can you match their job titles with the correct job descriptions?

Please do NOT write in this book if it is not yours. Use a separate piece of paper.

1. Uses wet cement to make foundation slabs, sidewalks, and roads
2. Drives big machinery like bulldozers and diggers at a construction site
3. Wires buildings for electricity
4. Designs buildings and creates blueprints showing how to build it
5. Designs outside spaces and parks for buildings and homes

A. Heavy equipment operator

B. Architect

C. Landscape architect

D. Concrete finisher

E. Electrician

Answer Key: 1-D; 2-A; 3-E; 4-B; 5-C

WHO? WHAT? WHERE?

Choose the correct job description to complete the sentences below:

1. An _____ designs and decorates the inside spaces of a building or home.
2. A _____ uses measurement tools to define the boundaries of a property.
3. A _____ uses a blowtorch to join pieces of metal together.
4. A _____ installs water and drainage pipes for kitchens and bathrooms.
5. A _____ cuts, installs, and seals glass in windows and skylights.

A. welder
B. plumber
C. interior designer
D. glazier
E. surveyor

Answer key: 1-C; 2-E; 3-A; 4-B; 5-D

CHAPTER 7
IT'S YOUR TURN

Hi there! It's me, Job. Now that you have read about my construction site adventures, it's your turn.

Share a story about a construction site you have seen. Be sure to mention all the people you saw doing different jobs.

Go online to download a free activity sheet at **www.cherrylakepublishing.com/activities**.

GLOSSARY

apprentice
person who learns how to do a job by helping an expert in the field

architect
expert who designs and creates drawings for buildings and homes

blowtorch
a small torch with an intense flame that is used to melt materials

blueprints
reproductions of technical drawings (not usually blue anymore)

brick mason
worker who uses bricks and concrete to build walls, walkways, fences, and more

concrete finisher
worker who places, finishes, seals, and repairs concrete

construction inspector
person who examines the building plans and construction site to make sure the builders are following codes and regulations

construction manager
person who oversees the process of constructing a building

construction worker
usually an unskilled worker who does much of the manual labor at a construction site

contractor
a specialist who is hired by a construction company to do a particular job

cost estimator
person who creates budgets and controls the money for construction projects

drafter
someone who turns drawings into blueprints

drywall installer
worker who installs drywall in rooms of a home or building

electrician
tradesman responsible for the electrical wiring of a building; installs electrical systems and fixes electrical problems

excavation manager
worker in charge of clearing a construction site so building can begin

finish carpenter
specialist who builds cabinets, doors, window frames, and decorative elements for a home or building

foundation
the stone or concrete structures that support a building from underneath

framer
a carpenter who builds the frame of a building using wood

glazier
specialist in cutting, installing, and sealing glass for unusually shaped windows, display cases, and more

heavy equipment operator
worker who operates large construction equipment such as cranes and bulldozers

interior designer
the person who designs the inside of a building or home

landscape architect
specialist who designs the outside spaces of a building, home, or school campus

landscaper
worker who plants bushes, trees, and other plants and maintains the outside of a building or home

painter
worker who paints walls and ceilings

paperhanger
worker who hangs wallpaper

permits
official documents giving someone permission to do something, such as construct a building

plumber
tradesman who installs and fixes water and drainage pipes for buildings and homes

rebar
metal rods used to strengthen concrete structures; also known as "reinforcing steel"

roofer
worker who specializes in building roofs

safety officer
person who makes sure all safety regulations are being met at a construction site

stone mason
person who works with stone to create walls, fireplaces, and more

surveyor
expert who uses measurement tools to make maps and set stakes so builders know the boundaries of where everything is to be built

trade school
secondary school that provides education and technical skills needed in order to perform the tasks of a particular job

welder
someone who specializes in welding, which is melting a metal base at high temperatures in order to connect metal pieces

INDEX

ABOUT THE AUTHOR

Joe Rhatigan is an accident-prone author whose works include *Ouch! The Weird & Wild Ways Your Body Deals with Agonizing Aches, Ferocious Fevers, Lousy Lumps, Crummy Colds, Bothersome Bites, Breaks, Bruises & Burns*; *White House Kids*; and *Inventions That Could Have Changed the World, But Didn't*. He lives in Asheville, North Carolina, with his wife and three kids.